Grammy Winners: A Decade of Music Excellence

Highlighting the Best Artists, Albums, and Moments in Grammy History

Elena Ellsworth

Disclaimer

This book is an independent publication and is not affiliated with, endorsed by, or sponsored by the Recording Academy or the Grammy Awards. All information is gathered from publicly available sources and is presented for informational and educational purposes only. The views and interpretations expressed in this book are solely those of the author and do not represent the official stance of the Grammy Awards or its organizers.

Table of Contents

Chapter 3: Grammy Winners of the Decade

- Celebrating the Artists Who Took Home the Gold
- Spotlight on Rising Stars and New Categories

Chapter 4: Best Albums of the Decade

- Top Grammy-Winning Albums and Their Cultural Impact
- Inside the Sound of Award-Winning Albums

Chapter 5: Memorable Grammy Moments

- Shocking Wins, Performances, and Controversies
- Iconic Stage Moments and Their Influence on Music

Chapter 6: Women Who Shaped Grammy History

- Female Artists Breaking Barriers and Winning Big
- The Role of Women in Changing the Grammy Landscape

Chapter 7: The Rise of Genre-Crossing Artists

- How Cross-Genre Collaboration Took Over the Grammy Scene
- Influential Genre-Bending Albums and Performances

Chapter 8: Grammy Controversies and Criticism

- Debates Over Nominations, Wins, and Snubs

- Key Statistics and Fun Facts

Introduction

The Grammy Awards, often called the "biggest night in music," have long been a symbol of recognition, prestige, and celebration within the music industry. Every year, this prestigious ceremony brings together the biggest stars in music, alongside rising talents, to showcase the very best in artistry, innovation, and influence. The Grammys, which started as a way to honor those who have shaped the musical landscape, have evolved into one of the most highly anticipated events in the entertainment calendar.

From unforgettable performances that give us goosebumps to surprise wins that spark debates, the Grammy Awards have created moments in history that resonate with music lovers around the world. But beyond the flashing cameras and red carpet glamour, the Grammys serve a deeper purpose: they acknowledge the power of music to move, inspire, and connect people across generations, cultures, and borders.

This book, *Grammy Winners: A Decade of Music Excellence*, takes you on a journey through the last decade of Grammy Award winners. It highlights the artists, albums, and moments that have defined a generation of music. From the rising stars to the legends who continue to push the boundaries of musical expression, we will explore what makes their achievements not just a testament to talent, but also a reflection of the cultural and social trends of their time.

We'll delve into the various categories, understanding the significance of each award, and how winning a Grammy can change the trajectory of an artist's career. Through this exploration, we aim to provide readers with a comprehensive look at how the Grammys have shaped, and continue to shape, the music industry.

A Brief History of the Grammy Awards

The Grammy Awards, formally known as the Gramophone Awards, were established by the National Academy of Recording Arts and Sciences (NARAS) in 1957. The inception of the Grammys was rooted in a desire to create a recognized institution that could honor the artistic excellence of the music industry. At that time, there was a growing recognition that music needed its own equivalent of Hollywood's Academy Awards, where the achievements of musicians, songwriters, and producers could be formally celebrated.

The first Grammy Awards ceremony took place in 1959, and it was a humble affair compared to the extravagant spectacle we see today. With only a handful of categories, the awards ceremony focused on recognizing the achievements of artists in fields such as classical, pop, jazz, and R&B. Among the first recipients were artists like Frank Sinatra, who took home the Best Male Vocal Performance award, and Ella Fitzgerald, who won Best Jazz Vocal

Performance. Over the years, the Grammys evolved, both in scope and significance, incorporating more categories to reflect the growing diversity of musical genres.

By the 1980s, the Grammys had firmly established themselves as the most important event in the music industry calendar. The televised ceremony began to attract millions of viewers globally, and winning a Grammy became an undeniable symbol of musical greatness. With the introduction of new categories such as Best Music Video and Best Dance/Electronic Album, the Grammys continuously adapted to reflect the changes in the industry, making it relevant for artists and fans alike.

Throughout its history, the Grammys have also been a reflection of societal changes, from acknowledging women's contributions to music to addressing issues of diversity and representation. Whether it's the way hip-hop and rap have risen to prominence or how Latin music has captured global attention, the Grammys have been there, witnessing and celebrating the evolution of music.

Today, the Grammy Awards have grown into an international institution. With over 80 categories, the event honors a wide array of genres, ranging from pop, rock, and country to classical, gospel, and even video game music. Artists from around the world now compete for this coveted recognition, and the ceremony itself has become a powerful platform for artistic expression, cultural conversations, and unforgettable moments in music history.

The Impact of the Grammys on the Music Industry

The Grammy Awards have had a profound influence on the music industry. For artists, winning a Grammy can be a career-defining moment, propelling them into the international spotlight and solidifying their legacy. But beyond the personal triumphs of individual winners, the Grammys also play a key role in shaping trends and the direction of the industry as a whole.

For many artists, the recognition that comes with winning a Grammy is the culmination of years of hard work, sacrifice, and artistic growth. A Grammy win can open doors to new opportunities, whether it's securing high-profile collaborations, booking larger concert tours, or gaining significant media attention. It can also lead to a surge in record sales and streaming numbers, as fans and casual listeners alike flock to discover the work of newly crowned Grammy winners. In many cases, a Grammy can help an artist transition from a niche following to mainstream stardom.

The Grammy Awards also have a significant impact on the music business side of the industry. For record labels, artists, and producers, the Grammy nominations and wins often influence marketing strategies, distribution decisions, and future investments in talent. In fact, the Grammy buzz is a crucial component in shaping the sales trajectory of albums and singles. Many artists and labels consider it a badge of honor to be associated with Grammy recognition, as it adds legitimacy and prestige to an artist's body of work.

On a broader scale, the Grammys often reflect and influence shifts in musical trends. The winners and nominees of any given year often represent the sounds, genres, and cultural movements that define the moment. For example, the rise of hip-hop and rap in the 2000s was mirrored by the Grammys' increasing recognition of the genre, culminating in the inclusion of several hip-hop-centric categories. In the past decade, Latin music has surged in popularity, with artists like Shakira, Bad Bunny, and J Balvin earning Grammy wins, showcasing how the Grammys are attuned to the global shifts in music tastes.

One of the most powerful aspects of the Grammys is their ability to create a platform for social change.

Over the years, artists have used their wins and performances as an opportunity to make bold statements on important social issues. Whether it's artists like Kendrick Lamar using the stage to raise awareness about racial inequality or Beyoncé's powerful celebration of Black culture, the Grammy Awards have given artists the opportunity to speak out on matters that matter. The ceremony has, in many cases, become a space for musicians to push the boundaries of art and activism, creating cultural moments that resonate far beyond the music industry.

Chapter 1: Defining Music Excellence

The Grammy Awards stand as the pinnacle of recognition in the music world. To win a Grammy is to receive acknowledgment from one's peers and the industry for outstanding achievement in music. But what does it truly mean to win a Grammy, and how do the awards evolve to represent the changing landscape of the music industry? In this chapter, we'll explore the essence of Grammy excellence and the major categories that have shaped the journey of music and its stars.

What Does It Mean to Win a Grammy?

To win a Grammy is to reach the pinnacle of artistic accomplishment. It signifies not only skill and dedication but also the ability to resonate with both the critics and the public in a way that few can. The

Grammy Award, in essence, is a reflection of both creativity and influence, and its prestige is built on decades of honoring the most remarkable contributions to the world of music.

1. Artistic Recognition: A Grammy win represents a clear acknowledgment from peers in the music industry, be it fellow artists, producers, or engineers. Unlike other awards that may be based on popularity or voting by the general public, the Grammys are judged by professionals who understand the nuances of music creation. These industry veterans assess the technical and artistic merit of each work, from the production value to the originality and emotional resonance of the music. A Grammy winner is seen as a true leader in their field, someone whose work stands out on a level that transcends trends.

2. Cultural Impact: Winning a Grammy often signifies that the artist or project has made a significant cultural impact. Music is a reflection of society, and Grammy-winning works often capture the essence of the moment in a unique way. Whether it's a song that became the anthem of a generation or an album that redefined a genre, the Grammy Awards honor works that influence and shape the cultural narrative.

3. Legacy and Career Defining: For many artists, winning a Grammy is a career-defining moment. It serves as a lasting acknowledgment of their contribution to music history. While not every deserving artist wins a Grammy, those who do often experience heightened visibility and longevity in their careers. This recognition can lead to increased sales, expanded fan bases, and future opportunities. Grammy-winning albums are often remembered not just as a product of their time but as milestones in the evolution of music.

4. A Symbol of Excellence: Finally, the Grammy statuette itself has become a symbol of excellence in music. It represents years of hard work, passion, and dedication to the craft. For both established and emerging artists, it's a milestone that carries immense prestige. The golden gramophone, iconic in its design, is an award that artists proudly display as a testament to their excellence.

Key Categories and Their Evolution

The Grammy Awards have grown significantly since their inception, with over 80 categories now being awarded annually. These categories span every imaginable genre and aspect of music production. However, they weren't always so diverse. In fact, the first Grammy Awards ceremony in 1959 featured only 28 categories. Over time, as music styles evolved and the industry grew, the Grammy categories expanded to accommodate new genres, trends, and technical advancements.

Let's take a closer look at some of the key Grammy categories and their evolution.

1. Record of the Year vs. Song of the Year: While both of these categories recognize excellence in music, they do so in distinct ways. The **Record of the Year** award honors the performance and production of a song, focusing on the artist's vocal or instrumental execution and the overall sound quality of the track. This award tends to emphasize the technical aspects of music, such as arrangement and engineering, along with the artist's performance.

On the other hand, the **Song of the Year** award honors the songwriter or lyricist behind the song. It focuses on the strength of the composition and the lyrical content. A song that resonates deeply with listeners or tackles a meaningful topic can win this award, even if it doesn't have the high-profile production quality of other tracks.

The distinction between these two categories is essential for recognizing both the artistry of the performer and the genius of the songwriter, allowing for broader recognition across the music industry.

2. Best New Artist: The **Best New Artist** category has consistently served as a springboard for up-and-coming talent. Traditionally, this award has given artists the recognition they need to break into the mainstream music scene. Over the years, the award has launched the careers of numerous stars, from Billie Eilish to Adele, who have gone on to dominate global music charts.

However, there has been debate over what constitutes a "new" artist. In some cases, artists who've been active for a few years and released multiple projects have won the award, while others who have made their major breakthroughs within the year of eligibility have been left out. The ever-evolving nature of the category reflects the changing dynamics of how music is consumed and promoted in the modern era, with social media, streaming platforms, and viral moments giving artists more ways to gain recognition.

3. Best Pop Vocal Album and Best Pop Solo Performance: As pop music continues to dominate charts worldwide, the Grammy categories dedicated to pop music have also grown in prominence. The **Best Pop Vocal Album** category is a recognition of an artist's full body of work in the pop genre, focusing on the strength of the album from a vocal performance and overall composition standpoint. It's a comprehensive award that looks at the artist's ability to craft an album that resonates with both critics and listeners.

Meanwhile, the **Best Pop Solo Performance** recognizes an individual performance of a song, typically by a solo artist. This category is reflective of an artist's ability to captivate with their voice and connect emotionally with listeners, often rewarding the most memorable and impactful vocal performances.

4. Best Rap Performance and Best Rap Album: The inclusion of hip-hop in the Grammy Awards was initially met with resistance, but over the decades, the genre has earned its rightful place as a dominant force in the industry. The **Best Rap**

Performance category honors a specific performance by an artist in the rap genre, while the **Best Rap Album** recognizes the best body of work in the genre. Both categories have grown in importance as hip-hop continues to shape mainstream music and culture, reflecting its undeniable influence across various mediums.

The evolution of these categories shows how the Grammys have responded to the rise of hip-hop as a leading genre in the global music scene. Artists such as Kendrick Lamar, Cardi B, and Travis Scott have been regular nominees and winners, illustrating the shifting taste in popular music and the Grammy's ability to adapt.

5. Best Latin Pop Album and Other Latin Music Categories: As Latin music has grown in global popularity, the Grammys have introduced specific categories to honor the best Latin albums and performances. The **Best Latin Pop Album** category acknowledges the best work in the Latin pop genre, celebrating artists who have managed to bring Latin sounds to the mainstream. Other categories like **Best Latin Rock or Alternative Album** and **Best Latin Urban Album** ensure that the diversity within Latin music is also recognized, further broadening the inclusivity of the Grammy Awards.

Chapter 2: A Look Back: The Decade in Music

The past two decades have witnessed unprecedented changes in the music industry. From technological innovations to shifting musical tastes, the sound of music has evolved in ways that no one could have predicted. The Grammy Awards, as a reflection of the music industry's best, have also evolved in response to these changes. In this chapter, we'll take a closer look at how the Grammy Awards have captured the trends, shifts, and global influences that have shaped music in the 2010s and 2020s.

Trends, Shifts, and the Changing Sound of the 2010s and 2020s

The 2010s and 2020s saw music undergo a transformation like never before. Technology, culture, and social movements all played significant roles in shaping the soundscape, leading to the rise of new genres, the blending of old and new styles, and the increasing dominance of digital platforms. The Grammy Awards mirrored these changes by expanding their categories and recognizing a wider range of musical styles.

1. The Rise of Streaming and Digital Music: The most profound shift in music during the past two decades has undoubtedly been the rise of streaming platforms like Spotify, Apple Music, and YouTube. In the early 2010s, music consumption was still largely centered around physical sales and digital downloads, but by the mid-decade, streaming became the dominant way people listened to music.

This shift also influenced how the Grammy Awards evaluated music. In the past, album sales were one of the key indicators of success, but now streaming numbers have become a major factor in an artist's eligibility for recognition. Tracks and albums that would have gone unnoticed in a previous era were propelled to the forefront, as streaming allowed for music to spread more widely and quickly than ever before.

Artists like Drake, Billie Eilish, and Post Malone saw massive success thanks to streaming platforms, which helped introduce their music to a global audience. The ability to reach millions of people instantly led to the rapid rise of new genres, such as trap, lo-fi hip hop, and electronic dance music, reshaping the Grammy landscape.

2. Genre Blending and the Emergence of New Styles: One of the defining trends of the past decade has been the blending of genres. In previous years, genres like pop, rock, country, and hip-hop were more distinct, with few artists straying too far from their roots. However, in the 2010s and 2020s, artists began to experiment more freely with genre fusion.

Pop stars like Taylor Swift and Ariana Grande embraced elements of R&B, electronic music, and hip-hop, while hip-hop artists like Travis Scott and Lil Nas X incorporated elements of rock and pop into their music. This fluidity between genres reflected the evolving tastes of music listeners, who were more inclined to embrace diverse sounds and styles.

Perhaps the most iconic example of genre-blending in the 2010s was Lil Nas X's "Old Town Road." The track fused country with hip-hop and became a global phenomenon. The song's success not only changed the way people thought about genre boundaries but also sparked a debate about the definition of country music and its place in the mainstream.

The Grammys responded to this shift by creating more inclusive categories that reflected the genre-blurring nature of modern music. The addition of new categories like **Best Rap/Sung Performance** and **Best Pop Duo/Group**

Performance allowed artists to be recognized for their innovative blends of genres, helping to bridge the gap between traditionally separate musical worlds.

3. The Dominance of Hip-Hop and R&B: In the 2010s, hip-hop and R&B emerged as the dominant genres on the charts, overshadowing pop and rock music. While the Grammy Awards have long recognized hip-hop, the 2010s marked a major turning point for the genre, with artists like Kendrick Lamar, Cardi B, and Childish Gambino receiving widespread acclaim and recognition.

Kendrick Lamar's "To Pimp a Butterfly" (2015) and "DAMN." (2017) not only solidified his place as one of the most influential artists of the decade but also brought socially conscious rap into the mainstream. The recognition of these albums at the Grammys represented a shift in the way hip-hop was perceived, acknowledging its ability to tackle complex themes such as race, inequality, and social justice.

R&B also experienced a resurgence during the 2010s, with artists like Frank Ocean, The Weeknd, and Solange pushing the boundaries of the genre. These artists' ability to blend soulful melodies with modern production techniques helped redefine R&B for a new generation of listeners.

The Grammy Awards mirrored this dominance by awarding several high-profile wins to hip-hop and R&B artists, including multiple wins for Kendrick Lamar, Billie Eilish, and Beyoncé, whose album **"Lemonade"** (2016) was celebrated for its cultural significance and genre-defying sound.

4. Social Movements and the Power of Music: The 2010s and 2020s were marked by significant social and political movements, and music played a crucial role in reflecting and amplifying these movements. From the Black Lives Matter movement to #MeToo and LGBTQ+ rights, artists used their music to address social issues and inspire change.

Songs like Childish Gambino's "This Is America" (2018), which highlighted issues of racial injustice, and Beyoncé's "Formation" (2016), which became an anthem for Black empowerment, showcased the ability of music to provoke conversation and challenge societal norms.

The Grammys began to recognize the cultural importance of such music, and in 2020, the ceremony even saw a historic moment when **Billie Eilish** swept the major categories, symbolizing a new era in music that was not only defined by talent but also by artists who spoke to the concerns and struggles of the world.

Global Influence: How the Grammys Have Evolved to Reflect the World

As music continues to become more globalized, the Grammy Awards have also evolved to reflect the broader, more diverse world of music. The increasing accessibility of music through digital platforms and the growing influence of international artists have made the Grammys more inclusive of different cultures, languages, and genres.

1. Expanding Categories to Reflect Global Music Trends: In response to the growing influence of international music, the Grammy Awards introduced several new categories to better represent diverse genres from around the world. For example, the addition of the **Best Latin Pop Album** and **Best Latin Rock/Alternative Album** categories in recent years was a direct acknowledgment of the enormous popularity of Latin music.

Similarly, the inclusion of awards such as **Best Global Music Album** and **Best African Music Performance** acknowledges the global reach of genres like Afrobeat, reggae, and K-pop. International artists like BTS, Burna Boy, and Rosalía have been nominated and awarded at the

Grammys, making the ceremony more representative of the global music landscape.

2. The K-Pop Phenomenon: One of the most significant global trends to emerge in the past decade has been the rise of K-pop, a genre that blends pop, hip-hop, R&B, and electronic dance music. With the success of groups like BTS, BLACKPINK, and EXO, K-pop has become a worldwide cultural phenomenon, reaching millions of fans across continents.

BTS's recognition at the Grammy Awards, including their nomination for **Best Pop Duo/Group Performance** in 2021 for "Dynamite," marked a milestone for K-pop, which had previously struggled to gain mainstream recognition in Western markets. The Grammy Awards' embrace of K-pop reflected the increasing influence of Asian music and culture on the global stage.

3. Acknowledging Non-English Language Music: In the past, the Grammy Awards were predominantly centered around English-language music, but as global music tastes have evolved, the Grammys have adapted. The success of Spanish-language music, particularly in the Latin and reggaeton genres, has forced the Grammys to reconsider their approach to non-English language music.

Artists like Bad Bunny, who became the first all-Spanish album to be nominated for **Album of the Year** with **"YHLQMDLG"** (2021), and Rosalía, whose album **"El Mal Querer"** received a Grammy for Best Latin Rock/Alternative Album, exemplify how the Grammys have opened the door for non-English-speaking artists to achieve recognition on a global scale.

Chapter 3: Grammy Winners of the Decade

The 2010s and 2020s marked a transformative era in music, with groundbreaking artists emerging across genres and pushing the boundaries of what it means to be recognized for musical excellence. From established superstars to breakthrough sensations, the Grammy Awards honored those who defined the sound of each year. In this chapter, we'll celebrate the Grammy winners of the decade—artists who not only took home the gold but also left an indelible mark on music history. We'll also shine a spotlight on rising stars and new categories that reflected the ever-changing landscape of the industry.

Celebrating the Artists Who Took Home the Gold

Every year, the Grammy Awards recognize the top talent across various genres, with winners earning the coveted Grammy trophy—a symbol of achievement, recognition, and success in the music industry. But over the course of the past decade, some artists truly stood out as monumental figures, not just in their genres, but in shaping the direction of music itself. Here, we highlight the iconic winners who made their mark during the 2010s and 2020s.

1. Billie Eilish: A Historic Sweep Billie Eilish's dominance in the 2020 Grammy Awards was nothing short of historic. At just 18 years old, Eilish became the youngest artist ever to win the four major categories: **Album of the Year, Record of the Year, Song of the Year, and Best New Artist**. Her debut album, *When We All Fall Asleep, Where Do We Go?*, not only took home these prestigious honors but also marked a shift in pop music toward a more introspective and minimalist sound. Billie's success at the Grammys was a reflection of her authentic approach to music and her influence on the pop landscape, creating music that resonates with a new generation of listeners.

**2. Kendrick Lamar: The King of Hip-Hop

Kendrick Lamar's influence on the music world in the 2010s is immeasurable. With albums like *To Pimp a Butterfly* (2015) and *DAMN.* (2017), Lamar not only redefined hip-hop but also used his platform to address pressing social issues such as race, inequality, and identity. His win for **Best Rap Album** in 2016 for *To Pimp a Butterfly* solidified his place as one of the most critically acclaimed and innovative artists of the decade. But Lamar's triumph wasn't just limited to his genre. In 2018, Lamar's "HUMBLE." won **Best Rap Song** and **Best Rap Performance**, marking a major milestone for hip-hop's recognition in mainstream music. He also made history in 2018 by winning the

Pulitzer Prize for Music, the first non-jazz, non-classical artist to ever do so.

3. Adele: The Reigning Pop Queen Adele's dominance in the 2010s was unmatched. Her soulful ballads and powerful voice captivated audiences worldwide. Her album *21* (2011) became a cultural phenomenon, and her Grammy sweep in 2012 for **Album of the Year, **Record of the Year**, and **Song of the Year** was a testament to her immense talent. But Adele's success wasn't just about winning trophies—her music resonated deeply with listeners who could relate to her heartfelt lyrics. In 2017, she continued to build on her legacy, winning **Album of the Year** again for *25*, while also inspiring an entire generation of artists with her raw, emotional performances.

**4. Taylor Swift: The Country-Pop Superstar Taylor Swift's career trajectory over the past decade has been nothing short of spectacular. Originally known for her country roots, Swift seamlessly transitioned into pop with albums like

1989 (2014) and *Reputation* (2017). With her ability to craft relatable songs and constantly evolve as an artist, Swift continued to reign at the Grammy Awards. Her win for **Album of the Year** for *1989* solidified her as one of the most influential figures in contemporary music. In 2021, Swift took home **Album of the Year** again for *Folklore*, showing her continued evolution and dominance in the industry.

5. Beyoncé: The Queen of Music Beyoncé is an artist who transcends categories, genres, and generations. Known for her unmatched vocal prowess, electrifying performances, and cultural influence, Beyoncé's achievements at the Grammys reflect her unparalleled legacy. In 2017, her album *Lemonade* was hailed as a groundbreaking work, blending pop, rock, R&B, and visual storytelling. Beyoncé's recognition at the Grammys culminated in her becoming the most-nominated female artist in Grammy history. In 2021, she made history by winning **Best R&B Performance** for "Black Parade," solidifying her as a true musical icon.

6. **Ed Sheeran: The Master of Melodies Ed Sheeran's rise to prominence in the 2010s was meteoric. With hits like "Shape of You" and "Thinking Out Loud," Sheeran became a pop sensation known for his catchy melodies and heartfelt lyrics. His Grammy win in 2016 for **Song of the Year** for "Thinking Out Loud" was a testament to his songwriting ability and his skill in connecting with listeners on an emotional level. Ed Sheeran's success in the 2010s was not just about hit singles; it was about his ability to craft timeless, relatable songs that resonated with fans across the globe.

Spotlight on Rising Stars and New Categories

While the established stars of the 2010s and 2020s undoubtedly made their mark, the Grammy Awards also spotlighted rising stars who brought fresh energy and innovation to the music scene. In addition, the creation of new categories over the past decade reflects the evolving nature of the music industry and its increasing inclusivity of diverse genres.

1. The Rise of K-Pop with BTS The rise of K-pop has been one of the most significant developments in global music over the past decade. With the meteoric success of groups like BTS and BLACKPINK, K-pop became a worldwide cultural phenomenon. BTS, in particular, made history by becoming the first K-pop group to be nominated for a Grammy in 2021 for their hit "Dynamite." Although they didn't win that year, their nomination marked a pivotal moment in the Grammys' recognition of international music. Their presence at the ceremony was a testament to the global nature of modern music, and their influence continues to grow year after year.

**2. The Emergence of Latin Music Stars
Latin music saw an explosion in popularity over the past decade, driven by artists like Bad Bunny, Rosalía, and J Balvin. These artists have not only brought Latin rhythms to mainstream music but have also used their platforms to advocate for cultural representation and unity. In 2021, Bad Bunny's *YHLQMDLG* made history by becoming the first all-Spanish album to be nominated for **Album of the Year**. This was a watershed moment for Latin music and its growing influence on global pop culture.

3. The Introduction of New Categories: Reflecting Music's Global Reach In response to the evolving music landscape, the Grammy Awards introduced several new categories to better reflect the diversity of musical styles and artists. The **Best Global Music Album category, introduced in 2020, was one such addition, recognizing the growing international influence of music from regions like Africa, Latin America, and Asia. Artists like Burna Boy, who won **Best Global Music Album** for *Twice as Tall* in 2021, exemplified the importance of this new category in honoring global music diversity.

Similarly, the **Best Latin Pop or Urban Album** category was created to acknowledge the growing dominance of Latin music, specifically in the pop and urban genres. These new categories not only highlight the diversity of contemporary music but also show how the Grammy Awards have adapted to represent an increasingly global and interconnected music industry.

4. Breakthrough Artists and the Changing Grammy Landscape Over the past decade, the Grammy Awards have also put a spotlight on breakthrough artists who have introduced new sounds and approaches to the music industry. Artists like Lizzo, who won **Best Pop Solo Performance** for "Truth Hurts," and Dua Lipa, who took home **Best New Artist** in 2019, exemplify how the Grammys have embraced emerging talent and fresh musical perspectives. These rising stars have not only won prestigious awards but have also played key roles in shaping the current sound of pop, R&B, and hip-hop.

Chapter 4: Best Albums of the Decade

The Grammy Awards are known for celebrating the top achievements in music, and among the most coveted awards is **Album of the Year**—a category that recognizes an artist's entire body of work within a single year. In this chapter, we'll explore the best albums of the decade, focusing on the Grammy-winning projects that defined musical tastes and left an indelible cultural mark. We'll also dive into the sounds that made these albums stand out, examining how they captured the essence of the times and resonated with audiences on a global scale.

Top Grammy-Winning Albums and Their Cultural Impact

The albums that took home **Album of the Year** at the Grammy Awards in the 2010s and 2020s are more than just collections of songs; they are reflections of their times, musical movements, and cultural moments. From groundbreaking debut albums to stunning reinventions, these albums became defining touchstones for an entire generation. Let's take a closer look at the top Grammy-winning albums from the past decade and their lasting cultural impact.

1. Adele - *21* (2012) Adele's *21* is a prime example of how an album can transcend musical boundaries and become a cultural phenomenon. Released in 2011, *21* took home **Album of the Year** in 2012, and for good reason. With heart-wrenching ballads like "Someone Like You" and "Rolling in the Deep," Adele's vulnerability and soulful delivery spoke to a wide audience, making her an international sensation. The album's themes of heartbreak and emotional recovery resonated universally, and it dominated charts for months, solidifying Adele's place as one of the most influential vocalists of her generation. *21* is an album that not only showcased Adele's immense talent but also redefined the power of traditional ballads in the modern pop era.

2. Taylor Swift - *1989* (2016) Taylor Swift's transition from country to pop was solidified with *1989*, which earned her the **Album of the Year** Grammy in 2016. The album, named after Swift's birth year, is a nostalgic and polished tribute to 80s-inspired synth-pop and a reimagining of her storytelling style. *1989* was a critical and commercial success, producing hits like "Shake It Off," "Blank Space," and "Bad Blood." Swift's embrace of pop music, paired with her skillful songwriting, allowed *1989* to become one of the decade's defining albums, influencing a whole generation of artists to blend catchy pop with personal narratives. Swift's ability to seamlessly transition between genres and continuously reinvent herself was celebrated with this win.

3. Kendrick Lamar - *DAMN*. (2018) In 2018, Kendrick Lamar's *DAMN*. made history by becoming the first non-jazz, non-classical album to win the **Pulitzer Prize for Music, adding to the Grammy-winning acclaim it already received. *DAMN*. marked a turning point in Lamar's career, showcasing his growth as both a poet and a musical innovator. The album touched on themes of faith, race, love, and struggle, with standout tracks like "HUMBLE." and "DNA." This powerful exploration of contemporary life and identity, coupled with Lamar's unparalleled lyricism and mastery over various musical styles, cemented *DAMN*. as one of the most influential albums of the decade. Lamar's Grammy win for **Best Rap Album** and **Album of the Year** was a victory not only for hip-hop but for the recognition of politically and socially conscious music in mainstream spaces.

4. Billie Eilish - *When We All Fall Asleep, Where Do We Go?* (2020) Billie Eilish's Grammy sweep in 2020 was nothing short of a cultural reset. *When We All Fall Asleep, Where Do We Go?* not only won **Album of the Year but also took home **Record of the Year**, **Song of the Year**, and **Best New Artist**. Eilish's debut album, co-produced with her brother Finneas, pushed the boundaries of pop and redefined the genre with its minimalistic production, eerie atmosphere, and introspective lyrics. Tracks like "Bad Guy" and "Everything I Wanted" resonated with listeners, particularly younger audiences who connected with Eilish's authentic and vulnerable approach to music. The album's dark, atmospheric sound, paired with its themes of mental health and self-discovery, made it a defining moment in the 2010s music scene, earning Eilish her place as a dominant force in pop music.

5. Jon Batiste - *We Are* (2022) Winning the **Album of the Year Grammy in 2022, Jon

Batiste's *We Are* was a celebration of American music and its history. Blending jazz, soul, pop, and R&B, Batiste created an album that was both a personal expression and a call to collective cultural action. The album's vibrant energy and political consciousness, paired with Batiste's virtuosic musicianship, made it one of the standout projects of the decade. "Freedom," one of the album's key tracks, became an anthem for empowerment, and its success at the Grammys was a testament to the growing recognition of artists who merge genres and use music as a tool for social change.

Inside the Sound of Award-Winning Albums

Behind every Grammy-winning album is a distinct sound that sets it apart from the rest. In this section, we'll take a closer look at the sonic elements and innovations that made these albums stand out in the ever-changing musical landscape of the past decade.

1. Adele - *21*: The Power of Raw Emotion
Adele's *21* is a masterclass in emotional storytelling through music. The album's instrumentation is minimalistic, with piano-driven ballads and subtle strings allowing Adele's powerhouse vocals to take center stage. Her ability to convey raw emotion through her voice—whether in the defiance of "Rolling in the Deep" or the vulnerability of "Someone Like You"—was one of the key elements that made *21* so impactful. The simplicity of the arrangements allowed Adele's voice to shine, and the album's timeless appeal lies in its universal themes of love, heartbreak, and healing.

2. Taylor Swift - *1989*: A Pop Revolution
1989 marked Taylor Swift's full embrace of the pop genre, and the album's sound was a revolution in itself. Drawing heavily on 80s synth-pop, *1989* incorporated sparkling synthesizers, infectious hooks, and upbeat rhythms, all while maintaining

Swift's signature lyrical vulnerability. Tracks like "Style" and "Wildest Dreams" showcased Swift's ability to craft melodic, earworm-worthy songs with deeply personal and reflective lyrics. The album's production, handled by Swift and collaborators like Max Martin and Shellback, created a sleek, polished sound that appealed to both pop purists and those looking for a fresh take on contemporary pop music.

3. Kendrick Lamar - *DAMN.*: A Genre-Defying Sound Kendrick Lamar's *DAMN.* was a genre-defying album that drew from a variety of musical influences, including hip-hop, jazz, rock, and electronic music. The production, led by Lamar and his team, was experimental yet accessible, with tracks like "Loyalty." featuring Rihanna blending lush instrumentation with hard-hitting beats. "DNA." and "HUMBLE." showcased Lamar's ability to deliver fierce, politically charged verses over minimalistic, bass-heavy production. What made *DAMN.* so special was Lamar's ability to combine powerful lyrical content with innovative soundscapes, creating an album that was not only musically diverse but also conceptually cohesive.

4. Billie Eilish - *When We All Fall Asleep, Where Do We Go?*: Minimalism Meets Eerie Pop Billie Eilish's debut album took the world by storm with its minimalist production and dark, atmospheric sound. The album's sparse arrangements, often featuring little more than bass and Eilish's breathy vocals, created a haunting atmosphere that felt simultaneously intimate and otherworldly. Eilish's brother, Finneas, co-produced the album, using a mix of electronic beats, lo-fi elements, and unconventional sounds to create a sonic landscape that was distinctly unique. This stripped-back, yet immersive sound, paired with Eilish's confessional lyrics, made the album stand out as one of the most innovative pop records of the decade.

5. Jon Batiste - *We Are*: A Fusion of Styles Jon Batiste's *We Are* is an exuberant celebration of the rich diversity of American music. The album combines elements of jazz, funk, soul, pop, and R&B, with a focus on creating joyful, danceable tracks that also carry deep social and political messages. The album's production is rich and dynamic, blending live instrumentation with electronic elements. Tracks like "Freedom" exude a celebratory energy, while others like "Cry" address more introspective themes. Batiste's musicality is evident in every song, and the album's eclectic nature captures the vibrancy and complexity of modern American music.

Chapter 5: Memorable Grammy Moments

The Grammy Awards are not just about celebrating the best music; they're also about unforgettable moments that capture the imagination of fans and leave a lasting mark on the cultural landscape. Over the years, the Grammys have been a stage for shocking wins, groundbreaking performances, and moments of controversy that sparked heated debates. From unexpected award winners to performances that pushed boundaries, the Grammy stage has become a theater for both triumph and drama.

In this chapter, we'll dive into some of the most memorable Grammy moments of all time, examining shocking wins, jaw-dropping performances, and controversies that captivated audiences. We'll also take a look at iconic stage moments and their long-term influence on the music industry and pop culture at large.

Shocking Wins, Performances, and Controversies

The Grammy Awards are often unpredictable, and the moments of shock and surprise are what make the ceremony so captivating. In this section, we'll explore some of the most shocking wins, bold performances, and controversial moments that made headlines in the world of music.

1. Beyoncé's Loss to Adele (2017) One of the most shocking Grammy moments of the 2010s came when Beyoncé's *Lemonade* lost **Album of the Year** to Adele's *25* in 2017. Many had predicted that *Lemonade*, widely considered a revolutionary album in terms of its themes of Black identity and empowerment, would take home the top prize. Beyoncé's performance during the show was powerful, yet Adele's more traditional pop album won the night. The internet exploded with reactions, and many argued that *Lemonade* deserved to win, given its cultural and political significance. Adele herself seemed conflicted, even expressing her admiration for Beyoncé and stating that *Lemonade* was the true winner. This moment highlighted the Grammy's struggle with representation and the cultural weight of different genres, especially when it comes to recognizing groundbreaking works.

2. Kanye West Interrupting Taylor Swift (2009) In one of the most infamous Grammy moments of all time, Kanye West interrupted Taylor Swift's acceptance speech for **Best Female Video** at the 2009 MTV Video Music Awards. Swift, who was just 19 at the time, was accepting her award for "You Belong With Me" when Kanye stormed the stage and declared that Beyoncé had the "best video of all time." The moment was an instant media frenzy, and Kanye received widespread criticism for his actions. The incident not only overshadowed Swift's win but also sparked a feud between the two artists that lasted for years. However, it also helped to elevate both artists' profiles—Swift became a victim of one of the most talked-about moments in pop culture, while Kanye's controversial actions only fueled his own notoriety. This event remains a defining moment in the intersection of celebrity, public relations, and the Grammy's broader cultural influence.

3. **Lady Gaga's "Meat Dress" (2010) Lady Gaga's Grammy appearance in 2010 included one of the most shocking outfits in the history of the award show: the infamous "meat dress." Designed by Franc Fernandez, the raw beef dress was a statement about the commodification of the human body, but it also left an indelible mark on pop culture. Gaga wore the dress to the 2010 MTV Video Music Awards, and it quickly became a symbol of her boundary-pushing, avant-garde approach to fashion and performance. Her Grammy win for **Best Pop Vocal Album** for *The Fame Monster* only added to the spectacle. The meat dress was talked about for months afterward, with some critics calling it a brilliant commentary on celebrity culture, while others decried it as a grotesque publicity stunt. Regardless of opinions, it cemented Lady Gaga as one of the most daring and unforgettable performers in Grammy history.

**4. The Controversial Snubbing of The Weeknd (2021) In 2021, The Weeknd's *After Hours* album, one of the biggest commercial successes of the year, was completely shut out of the Grammy nominations, despite dominating the charts and receiving critical acclaim. This decision sparked widespread backlash, with fans and music industry insiders questioning the credibility of the Grammy voting process. The Weeknd himself publicly criticized the Grammys, declaring that the system was rigged and claiming that the Recording Academy had "no transparency." The controversy led to conversations about the lack of diversity and fairness in the nomination process, with many feeling that The Weeknd's absence from the nominations was a glaring oversight. This incident fueled ongoing debates about the relevancy and fairness of the Grammys in the modern era.

5. Cardi B's Historic Win (2019) Cardi B's win for **Best Rap Album** at the 2019 Grammys was one of the most surprising and celebrated moments in recent Grammy history. Her album *Invasion of Privacy* made her the first solo female artist to win in this category, marking a significant achievement in a genre traditionally dominated by men. Cardi's win was seen as a breakthrough moment not only for women in hip-hop but also for the representation of Latinx and Afro-Latina artists in mainstream music. Her acceptance speech was emotional and heartfelt, as she thanked her family, fans, and the hip-hop community. The win also highlighted the changing face of hip-hop and the Grammy Awards' increasing recognition of diverse voices and perspectives.

Iconic Stage Moments and Their Influence on Music

The Grammy Awards are more than just an evening of accolades; they are a platform for unforgettable performances that push the boundaries of music and entertainment. Some Grammy performances have transcended the ceremony itself and become moments in music history. Let's take a look at some of the most iconic stage moments in Grammy history and explore their lasting influence on music.

1. Beyoncé's 2017 Grammy Performance (Lemonade) Beyoncé's performance at the 2017 Grammys, which was a tribute to her album *Lemonade*, is one of the most iconic moments in Grammy history. The performance was a breathtaking visual and musical spectacle that fused elements of African and African American culture with modern-day feminist and political themes. With stunning choreography and an all-female ensemble, Beyoncé paid tribute to Black culture, womanhood, and motherhood in a way that had never been done before at the Grammys. The performance's influence was felt long after the ceremony, sparking conversations about race, gender, and the power of visual storytelling in music. It helped solidify Beyoncé's status as not only a pop icon but also an activist and cultural leader.

2. **Prince's Tribute to George Harrison (2004) In 2004, Prince performed an unforgettable tribute to George Harrison, playing "While My Guitar Gently Weeps" during the **Grammy Lifetime Achievement Award** ceremony. Prince's virtuosic guitar solo became the stuff of legend, and the performance is considered one of the greatest live moments in Grammy history. The raw emotion and technical mastery Prince displayed while honoring Harrison's legacy left a lasting imprint on fans and musicians alike. This performance showcased the power of music to connect generations, honor legends, and push artistic boundaries.

3. Madonna's 2014 Grammy Performance (Living for Love) Madonna's performance of "Living for Love" at the 2014 Grammys was not only a visual spectacle but also a statement about reinvention and resilience. Dressed in a Matador-inspired outfit, Madonna performed the song surrounded by dancers dressed as bulls, symbolizing her fierce, unstoppable energy. The performance was both a nod to her long history of shocking and innovative performances and a celebration of her place in music history. It reminded audiences of her longevity and her ability to stay relevant while continually reinventing herself. This performance reinforced Madonna's position as one of the most influential pop stars of all time.

4. Shakira and Jennifer Lopez's 2020 Super Bowl Performance While not part of the Grammys themselves, the 2020 Super Bowl halftime show, which featured Shakira and Jennifer Lopez, had a massive influence on how women of color are represented in mainstream music. The performance, which took place just days before the Grammy Awards, was a celebration of Latin culture and empowerment, with both artists delivering high-energy performances that showcased their musical legacies and their cultural pride. The show's success resonated deeply in the Latinx community and was celebrated as one of the most memorable performances in the history of the event.

Chapter 6: Women Who Shaped Grammy History

Over the years, the Grammy Awards have recognized countless talented women who have not only achieved great success in the music industry but have also shaped the direction of popular culture. Female artists have broken barriers, shattered records, and altered the very landscape of music. Whether it's through groundbreaking performances, historic Grammy wins, or their role in advancing issues of gender, race, and diversity in music, women have always played a key role in the evolution of the Grammys.

This chapter will explore the significant contributions of female artists to the Grammy Awards, from those who have made history with their wins to those whose presence and influence have transformed the Grammy landscape. Through the stories of some of the most iconic women in music, we'll take a closer look at how women continue to break new ground in the industry and inspire future generations.

Female Artists Breaking Barriers and Winning Big

Women have been a central part of the Grammy Awards from its inception, but it hasn't always been easy for them to break into the upper echelons of the music industry. In the early years of the Grammys, female artists were often sidelined in categories dominated by men, or their contributions were dismissed in favor of male artists who were seen as more marketable. However, over time, women have proven that their talent, influence, and artistry are just as deserving of recognition as their male counterparts. Here are some notable women who have broken barriers at the Grammys.

1. Aretha Franklin – The Queen of Soul's Historic Wins Aretha Franklin, known as the "Queen of Soul," is one of the most awarded women in Grammy history. With 18 Grammy Awards, including a **Lifetime Achievement Award** and the **Best R&B Vocal Performance** for her iconic songs like "Respect" and "Think," Franklin was a pioneer in the music industry. She not only revolutionized soul music but also paved the way for future generations of female artists in genres like R&B, pop, and gospel. Her success at the Grammys, coupled with her powerful voice and unapologetic approach to music, made her a trailblazer for women in the music industry. Aretha's Grammy wins marked a historic moment in the recognition of female artists, cementing her legacy as one of the most influential musicians of the 20th century.

2. Beyoncé – A Record-Breaking Force in Music Beyoncé's influence on the Grammy Awards cannot be overstated. As of 2021, she has won 28 Grammy Awards, making her the most awarded female artist in Grammy history. Beyoncé has set numerous records, including being the first woman to win **Best R&B Performance** as a solo artist and the first female artist to receive the prestigious **Grammy Award for Best Contemporary R&B Album**. Her album *Lemonade* was hailed as a cultural milestone for Black women, addressing issues of race, identity, and empowerment. Beyond her Grammy wins, Beyoncé has used her platform to advocate for women's rights, racial justice, and LGBTQ+ rights, cementing her as one of the most powerful voices in music and beyond.

3. Taylor Swift – Changing the Game for Female Artists Taylor Swift's journey at the Grammys is a testament to her ability to reinvent herself and her music. As one of the youngest artists to ever win **Album of the Year** at the Grammys,

Swift has proven that she is a force to be reckoned with in both the country and pop genres. Her wins for albums like *Fearless*, *1989*, and *Folklore* have redefined what it means to be a successful woman in music. Taylor's ability to transition seamlessly from one musical genre to another has helped break down boundaries in the industry, challenging stereotypes about what type of music women can make. In 2021, Taylor Swift became the first woman to win **Album of the Year** three times, an achievement that reflects her consistent impact and influence on the music landscape.

4. Lady Gaga – Defying Norms and Pushing Boundaries Lady Gaga is one of the most avant-garde and genre-defying artists in the history of the Grammy Awards. Her breakthrough album, *The Fame*, not only revolutionized pop music but also established her as an artist who wasn't afraid to push the boundaries of both music and fashion. At the 2010 Grammys, Lady Gaga won **Best Dance Recording** for her hit song "Poker

Face," and she went on to win multiple awards for albums like *The Fame Monster* and *Born This Way*. Lady Gaga's commitment to creating music that challenges conventional gender roles, promotes LGBTQ+ visibility, and advocates for self-expression has made her a symbol of empowerment for women around the world. She is also an advocate for mental health awareness and women's rights, using her platform to support social justice causes.

5. Adele – Redefining Success for Women in Music Adele's rise to stardom was a game-changer for the music industry, particularly in the context of the Grammys. Her wins at the 2012 Grammy Awards, where she took home six awards, including **Album of the Year** for *21*, made her the most-awarded artist of the night and proved that women with raw, authentic talent could succeed on a global scale. Adele's career has been a testament to the power of voice and emotion, and her ability to connect with audiences through ballads about heartbreak and personal growth has set her apart from many of her contemporaries. As one of the most successful female artists of the 21st century, Adele has paved the way for women in music who refuse to conform to industry expectations.

The Role of Women in Changing the Grammy Landscape

Throughout the years, women have been instrumental in shaping the Grammy Awards. From trailblazing performances to setting new records, female artists have continually pushed the boundaries of what it means to be recognized at the highest level in music. But beyond their individual achievements, women have also played a pivotal role in shifting the culture of the Grammys and advocating for changes that reflect the evolving landscape of the music industry.

1. Advocating for Gender Equality and Representation In recent years, there has been growing concern about the lack of representation of women in certain categories at the Grammys, especially in genres like rock, country, and hip-hop. Female artists have used their platforms to call attention to this issue and advocate for greater diversity and gender equality in the nominations and voting processes. In 2018, for example, **Grammy nominee Lorde** called out the Recording Academy for not giving her a chance to perform solo at the ceremony despite being the only woman nominated in the **Album of the Year** category. Her remarks sparked discussions about the need for more women to be recognized and celebrated in the Grammy's top categories.

2. The #GrammysSoMale Movement One of the most powerful moments in the fight for gender equality at the Grammys came in 2018 with the **#GrammysSoMale** hashtag. After the male-dominated nominations for that year's

Grammy Awards sparked outrage, many artists, including **Kesha** and **Andra Day**, took to social media to call out the imbalance. The movement led to a much-needed conversation about the representation of women in music and the need for the Grammy Awards to recognize a wider diversity of voices, particularly those of female musicians and artists of color. The conversation ignited efforts by the Recording Academy to diversify its membership, ensuring that more female and minority voices were involved in the voting process.

3. Women at the Helm of Music Labels and Production Women have also made waves in the business side of the music industry, particularly in areas like music production and label management. Female producers, like **Sylvia Robinson**, **Missy Elliott**, and **Linda Perry**, have made significant contributions to shaping the sound of popular music and breaking the gender barriers that have historically existed in music production. In addition, women like **Shirley Halperin** and **Joan**

Jett have played crucial roles in the creation of some of the most iconic moments in Grammy history, both onstage and behind the scenes.

**4.   Female-Dominated   Collaborations
Another key shift has been the increasing number of collaborations between female artists in various genres. Artists like **Cardi B**, **Nicki Minaj**, and **Megan Thee Stallion** have teamed up to create tracks that highlight the power of women in hip-hop, pop, and R&B. These collaborations have created new opportunities for women in music to share the stage and push each other to new heights. With female artists supporting and amplifying one another, they continue to transform the Grammy Awards, making it a more inclusive space for all voices.

Chapter 7: The Rise of Genre-Crossing Artists

Over the past decade, the Grammy Awards have witnessed an exciting evolution in the landscape of music. One of the most noticeable trends has been the rise of genre-crossing artists—musicians who blur the lines between traditional genres and experiment with different styles, sounds, and influences. These genre-bending artists have become some of the most exciting figures in the music industry, pushing boundaries, reshaping the Grammy stage, and challenging traditional notions of genre.

Gone are the days when artists were confined to a specific musical style or genre. Today, artists are mixing elements of rock, pop, hip-hop, R&B, country, jazz, electronic, and more, creating unique soundscapes that reflect the diversity of contemporary musical tastes. The Grammy Awards, once known for honoring artists within rigid genre categories, have had to adapt and celebrate this innovative shift in the industry.

This chapter explores the rise of genre-crossing artists, how cross-genre collaboration has taken over the Grammy scene, and the influential albums and performances that have shaped the sound of modern music. From genre-defying performances to groundbreaking albums, genre-crossing artists are undeniably reshaping the Grammy landscape.

How Cross-Genre Collaboration Took Over the Grammy Scene

In the past decade, the notion of genre has become increasingly fluid in the music world, especially as more artists experiment with blending diverse styles. The Grammys, known for their rigid genre categories, have found themselves accommodating this shift as cross-genre collaborations have become a central part of the music industry. Here's how these collaborations have reshaped the Grammy stage.

1. The Explosion of Cross-Genre Collaborations One of the most exciting developments in recent years has been the rise of collaborations that fuse multiple genres. This trend can be seen across every major music genre, with artists from different backgrounds coming together to create fresh sounds that appeal to a broad audience. The Grammy Awards have increasingly celebrated these collaborations, recognizing the creativity and diversity that come from genre-blending. Take, for example, the hit collaboration between **Lil Nas X** and **Billy Ray Cyrus** on "Old Town Road," which blends country and rap. This song broke records, dominating the charts and ultimately winning a **Grammy for Best Music Video**.

Another groundbreaking moment came when **Cardi B** and **Megan Thee Stallion** collaborated on "WAP." The track blends hip-hop and pop influences with its bold lyrics and provocative beat, and it became one of the most discussed songs of the year. Their performance at the 2021 Grammy Awards was a cultural moment, showing the power of cross-genre collaborations in both music and performance.

2. Genre-Bending Albums and the Changing Nature of Nominations As artists experiment with blending genres, albums are increasingly reflecting this evolution. One of the most remarkable shifts has been the rise of albums that defy categorization. Take **Billie Eilish's** *When We All Fall Asleep, Where Do We Go?*, which blends elements of pop, electronic, indie, and alternative music. This genre-bending album was not only a commercial success but also received critical acclaim, winning multiple Grammys, including **Album of the Year**.

Similarly, **Post Malone's** *Hollywood's Bleeding* incorporates a mix of hip-hop, rock, and pop. This genre-blending album was praised for its diversity and earned Post Malone **Grammy nominations** for Best Pop Vocal Album and **Record of the Year** for "Circles."

The Grammys have adapted to this trend by creating more flexible categories and encouraging genre-blending in their nominations. In recent years, we've seen categories like **Best Pop Duo/Group Performance** and **Best Rock Performance** include artists who push the boundaries of their respective genres, showcasing how diverse and fluid the music landscape has become.

3. The Growing Impact of Streaming Platforms Streaming platforms like Spotify, Apple Music, and YouTube have played a significant role in the rise of genre-crossing artists. These platforms offer a wider range of music to listeners, breaking down barriers between genres and creating a more interconnected musical world. As a result, artists are no longer restricted to one genre or type of audience—they can experiment with different sounds and reach listeners from all over the world.

With the rise of algorithms that suggest new music based on user preferences, listeners are exposed to a diverse range of artists and genres, influencing the kind of music that's being created and consumed. The accessibility of various genres allows genre-crossing artists to flourish, leading to collaborations that would have been less likely to happen in the past.

Influential Genre-Bending Albums and Performances

Now that cross-genre collaboration has become a hallmark of the music industry, let's look at some of the most influential genre-bending albums and performances that have not only reshaped the Grammy Awards but also influenced the broader musical culture.

1. Childish Gambino – *This Is America* One of the most groundbreaking genre-blending moments in recent Grammy history came with **Childish Gambino's** "This Is America." The song, which fuses elements of hip-hop, trap, R&B, and gospel, became a cultural and political statement. Its accompanying music video, which juxtaposes vibrant dance choreography with stark images of violence, sparked widespread discussions on race, gun violence, and social justice.

At the 2019 Grammy Awards, "This Is America" won **Song of the Year**, **Record of the Year**, and **Best Rap/Sung Performance**—a testament to how the track crossed genre boundaries to make an impact both musically and politically. The success of this track not only demonstrated the power of genre-blending but also solidified **Donald Glover** as one of the most influential artists of the decade.

2. Kacey Musgraves – *Golden Hour* In 2019, **Kacey Musgraves** made history by winning **Album of the Year** for her album *Golden Hour*, an album that masterfully blends country, pop, and psychedelic influences. Musgraves' blend of these genres helped redefine what country music could be in the 21st century, and her success at the Grammys showed that genre boundaries were no longer as rigid as they once were. *Golden Hour* was hailed as one of the best albums of the decade, thanks to its bold experimentation and the way it merged different musical styles.

Kacey Musgraves' Grammy success was a turning point for country music, which had often been seen as stuck in its traditional roots. Her win signaled that genre-crossing albums were not only welcome at the Grammys, but could also be highly acclaimed.

3. The Weeknd – *After Hours* and the Fusion of R&B, Pop, and Electronic The Weeknd's *After Hours* is a shining example of genre-blending that combines R&B, pop, and electronic music. The album's chart-topping single, "Blinding Lights," is a prime example of how genre-crossing artists are redefining the boundaries of popular music. With its retro synth-pop sound, "Blinding Lights" became one of the biggest hits of 2020, and its success at the Grammys further cemented **The Weeknd's** status as one of the most influential genre-bending artists of his generation.

Although *After Hours* was critically acclaimed, the lack of nominations for **Album of the Year** or **Record of the Year** at the 2021 Grammy Awards sparked controversy and conversations about how genre-blending albums are sometimes overlooked in favor of more traditional releases. Nevertheless, The Weeknd's success on the charts and in popular culture exemplified the growing trend of genre-crossing music in the modern era.

4. Lil Nas X – *Montero* and the Fusion of Country, Rap, and Pop Lil Nas X shook the world in 2019 with his hit song "Old Town Road," a track that blended country and rap in a way that no one had expected. The song's success on the charts and at the Grammys was a defining moment in the rise of genre-bending music. Lil Nas X didn't just break records—he broke down barriers, showing that genres didn't need to be mutually exclusive.

In 2021, Lil Nas X's album *Montero* pushed the boundaries even further, blending pop, rap, and country elements into an album that explores themes of self-acceptance, sexuality, and identity. The album's success at the Grammys reflected how genre-crossing artists are increasingly embraced by the mainstream, marking a significant moment in the changing nature of the music industry.

Chapter 8: Grammy Controversies and Criticism

The Grammy Awards, widely regarded as one of the most prestigious honors in the music industry, have not been immune to their share of controversies and criticisms. While the Grammys celebrate the best in music, their decisions, nominations, and outcomes often spark debates, dissatisfaction, and even scandal. The awards have faced backlash from artists, fans, and industry professionals, all questioning the validity, fairness, and transparency of the process.

In this chapter, we explore the various controversies that have rocked the Grammys, from heated debates over nominations and wins to the infamous snubs that have left fans and artists outraged. We also take a closer look at some of the most talked-about Grammy scandals, their aftermath, and how they have shaped the reputation of the awards in the eyes of the public and the music industry.

Debates Over Nominations, Wins, and Snubs

At the heart of Grammy controversies are the debates surrounding the nominations, wins, and snubs. The Grammy process, which involves voting by members of the National Academy of Recording Arts and Sciences (NARAS), has often been criticized for a lack of transparency, and for favoring established artists over emerging talent. Here are some of the key issues that have fueled these debates:

1. The "Snubbing" of Artists: Who Gets Left Out? One of the most common sources of controversy at the Grammys is the phenomenon of "snubs"—when highly anticipated artists or albums are overlooked in favor of others. These snubs can be particularly shocking when the artist has had a major impact on the music industry that year, or when their work is widely regarded as groundbreaking or innovative.

The Weeknd's 2021 Snub:

One of the most talked-about snubs in recent Grammy history occurred in 2021, when **The Weeknd's** critically acclaimed album *After Hours* and its massive hit "Blinding Lights" were completely shut out of the nominations. Despite the album's commercial success, popularity, and critical acclaim, The Weeknd did not receive a single nomination at the 63rd Annual Grammy Awards. The decision sparked outrage among fans and industry professionals, with many accusing the Grammys of overlooking one of the most influential artists of the year. **The Weeknd** himself voiced his frustration on social media, saying that the Grammys were "corrupt" and that their decision-making process was flawed.

The Beyoncé and "Lemonade" Controversy: Another major snub that fueled Grammy debates was the exclusion of **Beyoncé's** 2016 album *Lemonade* from winning the prestigious **Album of the Year** category. Despite receiving widespread acclaim and becoming a cultural touchstone, *Lemonade* lost out to **Adele's** *25*, which many fans and critics believed was not as groundbreaking. The outcome ignited debates over race, gender, and the Grammy voting process, as *Lemonade* was considered by many to be one of the most innovative and influential albums of the decade.

2. The "Bias" Against Certain Genres and Artists The Grammys have long been accused of exhibiting bias against certain genres, particularly hip-hop and R&B. Despite the immense popularity and influence of these genres, they have often been underrepresented in the major categories like **Album of the Year** and **Song of the Year**. Hip-hop, in particular, has faced criticism for being relegated to secondary categories, while more mainstream genres like pop and rock have dominated the major categories.

In 2019, **Kendrick Lamar's** *DAMN.* album won **Best Rap Album**, but despite being hailed as one of the best albums of the year, it was not nominated for **Album of the Year**, an oversight that many considered a reflection of the Grammy's bias against hip-hop. The controversy reached its peak when **Kendrick Lamar** became the first hip-hop artist to win the **Pulitzer Prize for Music** in 2018, yet was still overlooked for the Grammy's top honors.

3. Lack of Diversity in the Voting Process
Another ongoing criticism of the Grammys is the lack of diversity among its voting body. While the National Academy of Recording Arts and Sciences (NARAS) claims to represent the diversity of the music industry, many artists and advocates argue that the Grammy voting membership lacks sufficient representation from communities of color, women, and other underrepresented groups.

This lack of diversity has raised questions about whether the Grammy Awards truly reflect the broad spectrum of talent in the music world.

In 2020, the controversy reached new heights when **Grammy CEO Deborah Dugan** alleged that the Grammy Awards were plagued by corruption and biases in the voting process. Dugan claimed that the voting body was influenced by outside pressures, such as favoritism, financial interests, and industry politics, rather than an objective assessment of musical merit. The ensuing investigation into her claims led to further revelations about the lack of transparency in the Grammy process.

A Closer Look at Grammy Scandals and Their Aftermath

While the debates over nominations and snubs are always intense, the Grammys have also been embroiled in several scandals that have had lasting repercussions. These scandals often involve unethical behavior, controversial statements, or situations that call into question the integrity of the award show. Here are some of the most notable scandals in Grammy history:

1. The 1989 Grammy Controversy: Milli Vanilli's Award Revoked One of the most infamous scandals in Grammy history occurred in 1990 when the duo **Milli Vanilli** had their Grammy Award for **Best New Artist** revoked after it was revealed that they had not actually sung on their album. Instead, **Fab Morvan** and **Rob Pilatus** had lip-synced to vocals recorded by other singers. The revelation rocked the music industry and led to a public backlash against the Grammys for not properly vetting the winners. The scandal raised questions about the integrity of the Grammy voting process and the standards by which artists are recognized.

2. The 2014 "Rap Music is Not Real Music" Scandal In 2014, the Grammy Awards faced criticism when **Macklemore & Ryan Lewis** won the **Best Rap Album** award for *The Heist* over **Kendrick Lamar's** *good kid, m.A.A.d city,* which was widely considered to be the superior album. Many felt that the Grammy's decision to award Macklemore, a white rapper, over Lamar, a black rapper, was an example of institutional racism. The controversy deepened when **Macklemore** posted an apology to Kendrick Lamar on social media, acknowledging that Lamar deserved the award.

This incident fueled ongoing debates about the Grammy's treatment of hip-hop and raised questions about racial bias in the awards. It also highlighted the increasing tension between mainstream and underground music scenes, as Lamar's album was seen as a more authentic and influential representation of the genre.

3. The #GrammysSoWhite Movement In 2016, the hashtag **#GrammysSoWhite** went viral after the Grammy Awards were accused of being racially biased, following a lack of African American nominees in major categories. While artists like

Kendrick Lamar and **The Weeknd** were recognized in the rap and R&B categories, they were once again overlooked in the **Album of the Year** and **Song of the Year** categories. This sparked widespread protests against the Grammy Awards, with many artists, including **The Weeknd**, **Frank Ocean**, and **Janelle Monáe**, speaking out against the lack of diversity in the nominations.

The backlash led to significant changes within the Academy, with the introduction of new initiatives aimed at diversifying the voting body and increasing representation for underrepresented groups. Despite these efforts, the issue of diversity and inclusion remains a contentious topic at the Grammys.

Chapter 9: The Future of the Grammys

The Grammy Awards have stood as the pinnacle of recognition for artistic achievement in the music industry for more than six decades. Since their inception, the Grammys have evolved significantly, adapting to changes in the music landscape, technology, and society at large. However, with the rapid advancements in music production, distribution, and consumption, the question arises: **Will the Grammy Awards continue to evolve?**

As the music industry faces challenges related to digital disruption, globalization, and shifting cultural dynamics, the Grammys must adapt to stay relevant in a rapidly changing world. In this chapter, we will explore the future of the Grammys, examining the challenges the awards face, the changes that might occur, and predictions for the next decade of music excellence.

Will the Grammy Awards Continue to Evolve?

The short answer is yes—the Grammys will almost certainly continue to evolve, as they have since their creation. However, the process of evolution is complex, and the direction of change depends on several factors, including technological advancements, cultural shifts, and industry pressures. Let's explore how the Grammys are likely to evolve and the challenges they face in the coming years.

1. Embracing Digital Platforms and Streaming Services The rise of digital platforms and streaming services has radically transformed how people consume music. In the past, Grammy nominations and wins were largely determined by traditional album sales, radio play, and industry influence. Today, streaming services like **Spotify**, **Apple Music**, and **YouTube** are the dominant platforms for music discovery, which poses a challenge for the Grammys as they adjust to the streaming era.

To remain relevant, the Grammys will need to better integrate streaming data into the nomination process. Some changes have already been made—such as including **streaming metrics** in the decision-making process for categories like **Song of the Year** and **Best New Artist**—but the full integration of digital platforms into the Grammys' system will likely continue in the future.

2. Transparency and Accountability in the Voting Process One of the key criticisms of the Grammy Awards over the years has been the lack of transparency in the voting process. Despite the National Academy of Recording Arts and Sciences (NARAS) implementing some changes to address this, critics argue that the process remains opaque and that the public still doesn't know enough about how votes are cast or who is actually doing the voting.

To address this concern and maintain credibility, the Grammys will likely need to introduce more transparent practices. This could include revealing more information about the voting body, the weight of votes, and even introducing public voting or fan participation in certain categories. **Public trust** is essential for the Grammy Awards to continue to be seen as a fair and legitimate recognition of artistic excellence.

3. Adapting to Globalization and Diverse Genres The Grammy Awards have historically been centered around the U.S. music industry, but as globalization continues to reshape the music landscape, it's clear that the Grammys must expand their scope to reflect global diversity. Genres that once felt niche or peripheral, such as **Afrobeats**, **K-Pop**, and **Latin music**, have gained tremendous popularity in recent years. Artists from regions like Africa, South America, and Asia have become global superstars, making it imperative for the Grammys to evolve to reflect this shift.

Already, we've seen the inclusion of **Best Latin Pop or Urban Album** and **Best Global Music Album** categories. Expect to see more categories that recognize the influence of international genres, as well as collaborations between artists from different parts of the world.

4. The Role of Artificial Intelligence and Technology in Music Production The rapid development of artificial intelligence (AI) and technology is revolutionizing the music industry. AI-driven tools are now being used to create music, analyze trends, and even generate lyrics. This evolution of technology could impact how Grammy nominations are determined, particularly in categories like **Best New Artist** and **Album of the Year**, as AI could play a more prominent role in both the production and discovery of music.

However, the potential challenges of AI in music raise several ethical concerns. For example, if AI-generated music gains recognition at the Grammys, how will the industry respond to questions about artistic authenticity? Will the Grammys be able to navigate this shift in a way that honors both human creativity and technological innovation? These are questions that will likely be addressed in the coming decade.

Predictions for the Next Decade of Music Excellence

With the pace of change accelerating in the music industry, it's difficult to predict exactly how the Grammy Awards will look in the next decade. However, based on current trends and industry dynamics, several key predictions can be made.

1. Rise of Cross-Genre Categories As music continues to blur the lines between genres, the Grammys will likely introduce more **cross-genre categories** to reflect the growing trend of genre fusion. We've already seen the rise of genre-bending artists, such as **Lil Nas X, Billie Eilish**, and **Kanye West**, who defy easy classification into traditional categories like pop, rock, or rap. Expect to see categories like **Best Genre-Bending Album** or **Best Hybrid Performance** to accommodate artists who incorporate multiple genres into their music.

2. Expanded Focus on Streaming Metrics and Data Analytics As streaming services continue to dominate the music industry, the Grammys will increasingly incorporate streaming data into the decision-making process. In the near future, the **Billboard Hot 100** charts, **Spotify streams**, and **YouTube views** could play an even larger role in determining Grammy nominations. This could help the awards better reflect the **current listening habits** of music fans, as well as the rise of viral songs and trends that might not be captured by traditional album sales.

3. Greater Representation of Underrepresented Groups Diversity and inclusion will likely continue to be a major focus in the coming decade. The Grammy Awards have been under pressure to improve representation, not only in terms of race and ethnicity but also gender, sexual orientation, and other underrepresented groups. As the music industry becomes more inclusive, the Grammys will need to prioritize recognizing talent from all corners of society, from women and LGBTQ+ artists to people of color and other marginalized communities.

4. More Collaboration Between the Grammys and Fans Given the increasing power of **social media** and **fan-driven culture**, the Grammys may find new ways to engage with fans, perhaps even allowing fans to participate in the nomination or voting process in certain categories. **Fan-voted awards** are becoming more common in the entertainment industry (e.g., the **People's Choice Awards**), and it wouldn't be surprising if the Grammys followed suit with a similar initiative, allowing fans to cast votes for their favorite nominees in real-time.

5. Environmental Sustainability and Ethical Music Practices As the world becomes more aware of environmental issues, the music industry is also evolving to address sustainability. The next decade could see the Grammys implement more **eco-friendly practices** in their ceremonies, such as reducing carbon footprints, promoting sustainable fashion, and ensuring that the event itself is powered by renewable energy sources. Additionally, the conversation around **ethical music practices**, such as fair compensation for artists and the role of streaming platforms in artist revenue, will likely become more central to the Grammy discourse.

Conclusion: The Enduring Influence of the Grammys on Music Culture

The **Grammy Awards** have long been a symbol of music's highest achievement, but as the industry continues to evolve, the relevance and future of the Grammys remain a topic of much discussion. The question we must ask is: How will the Grammys continue to shape and influence the music culture of the future?

How the Grammys Will Continue to Influence Music Culture

The Grammy Awards' impact extends far beyond the night of the ceremony itself. These awards hold immense cultural weight, often shaping how we perceive the artists, albums, and songs that define a given era. As we look to the future, the Grammys will undoubtedly continue to influence music culture in several key ways:

1. Shaping Trends and Defining the Sound of an Era

Throughout history, Grammy wins have highlighted the most important and influential musical movements, cementing them in history. For instance, the recognition of artists like **Bob Dylan**, **Madonna**, and **Beyoncé** has directly influenced how we think about genres, musical innovation, and cultural impact. Moving forward, the Grammys will continue to spotlight emerging genres, including **Afrobeats**, **Latin trap**, and **hyperpop**, that are likely to define the music landscape of the 2020s and beyond.

By recognizing the best artists and albums in each genre, the Grammys continue to create a **barometer of musical excellence** that helps the industry and fans identify where music is headed. The awards, in turn, encourage artists to push the boundaries of creativity in their work, which, in turn, leads to a more dynamic and exciting cultural exchange across the globe.

2. Bridging Generational Gaps

The Grammys are one of the few institutions where both **new artists** and **musical legends** are celebrated on the same stage. The awards ceremony often brings together artists from various generations, allowing for cross-generational collaborations and exchanges that promote understanding and mutual respect. This tradition of honoring diverse talent from across eras helps bridge the gap between younger, experimental artists and established superstars.

For instance, collaborations like **Dua Lipa** with **Elton John** or **Lil Nas X** with **Billy Ray Cyrus** not only boost the profile of both artists but also allow for the merging of styles from different periods, giving audiences a more holistic sense of the diverse range of musical influences. This synergy helps both new and older generations see their own musical taste reflected in the same space, ensuring that **the Grammy Awards remain a living institution** that acknowledges both the past and future of music.

3. Cultural Conversations and Social Justice

The Grammys are uniquely positioned to drive cultural conversations, often reflecting and amplifying societal concerns. Over the years, Grammy winners have made bold statements about **social justice**, **gender equality**, and **mental health**. As the world becomes more conscious of these issues, the Grammys will likely continue to be a space for political commentary and activism, with artists using the platform to advocate for change.

For example, artists like **Beyoncé** and **Kendrick Lamar** have used their Grammy performances to raise awareness about **racial inequality**, while others like **Billie Eilish** and **Lady Gaga** have addressed mental health through their music and speeches. As the cultural landscape evolves, the Grammys will continue to provide an important stage for artists to address the pressing issues of our time.

The Ongoing Legacy of Grammy Winners

The lasting legacy of the Grammy Awards is woven into the fabric of music history. Artists who win Grammy Awards become part of a prestigious legacy that continues to influence future generations of musicians and music fans. Here's how the Grammy legacy endures:

1. Defining Artist Careers

For many artists, a **Grammy win** is the ultimate recognition of their creative achievements. It often marks a turning point in an artist's career, opening doors to new opportunities, larger audiences, and increased visibility. Winners of Grammy Awards often experience a significant boost in their careers, with their work being viewed as the gold standard in their genre. For example, winning **Album of the Year** can elevate an artist's career from niche popularity to global stardom, as seen with **Adele**, **Taylor Swift**, and **Kendrick Lamar**.

Beyond career growth, winning a Grammy also has profound effects on an artist's **legacy**. Artists who win multiple Grammys, such as **Beyoncé** and **Stevie Wonder**, are often regarded as cultural icons whose contributions are acknowledged far beyond the music world.

2. Cementing Albums as Cultural Landmarks

The albums that win **Album of the Year** often go on to become cultural landmarks, influencing future musicians, shaping public discourse, and reflecting the mood of a specific time in history. Albums like **Michael Jackson's "Thriller"**, **Adele's "21"**, and **Beyoncé's "Lemonade"** are not just celebrated for their musicality but are deeply ingrained in the cultural zeitgeist. These albums are still referenced years or even decades later, as they continue to influence music, fashion, politics, and beyond.

Winning a Grammy allows artists to cement their place in **music history**, and their work becomes part of a larger conversation about culture and identity. It's not just about the accolades but about what the album or artist represents within a broader context.

3. The Impact of Grammy-Winning Collaborations

The legacy of Grammy-winning collaborations continues to shape the direction of music. Pairings between artists from different genres often produce some of the most innovative and influential work of the decade. The continued success of collaborations—such as **Shakira** and **Jennifer Lopez** at the 2020 Grammy Awards—shows how artists from different musical backgrounds can come together to create memorable moments that leave a lasting impact on both the industry and fans.

Collaborations at the Grammys often push boundaries and set new trends, making them pivotal moments in the evolution of contemporary music.

Appendix: Complete List of Grammy Winners (2010-2020)

The following list highlights the **Grammy Award winners** from 2010 to 2020 across some of the most prominent categories. These include the coveted **Album of the Year**, **Song of the Year**, and **Record of the Year**, along with some genre-specific categories that reflect the diversity and richness of the music scene over the past decade.

2010

- **Album of the Year**: "Fearless" – Taylor Swift

- **Song of the Year: "Single Ladies (Put a Ring on It)"** – Beyoncé
- **Record of the Year: "Use Somebody"** – Kings of Leon
- **Best New Artist: Zac Brown Band**
- **Best Pop Vocal Album: "The E.N.D."** – The Black Eyed Peas

2011

- **Album of the Year: "The Suburbs"** – Arcade Fire
- **Song of the Year: "Need You Now"** – Lady Antebellum
- **Record of the Year: "Rolling in the Deep"** – Adele
- **Best New Artist: Esperanza Spalding**
- **Best Pop Vocal Album: "The Fame Monster"** – Lady Gaga

2012

- **Album of the Year: "21"** – Adele

- **Song of the Year: "Rolling in the Deep"** – Adele
- **Record of the Year: "Somebody That I Used to Know"** – Gotye featuring Kimbra
- **Best New Artist: Bon Iver**
- **Best Pop Vocal Album: "Strong"** – Kelly Clarkson

2013

- **Album of the Year: "Babel"** – Mumford & Sons
- **Song of the Year: "We Are Young"** – Fun. featuring Janelle Monáe
- **Record of the Year: "Somebody That I Used to Know"** – Gotye featuring Kimbra
- **Best New Artist: The Lumineers**
- **Best Pop Vocal Album: "Stronger"** – Kelly Clarkson

2014

- **Album of the Year**: **"Random Access Memories"** – Daft Punk
- **Song of the Year**: **"Royals"** – Lorde
- **Record of the Year**: **"Get Lucky"** – Daft Punk featuring Pharrell Williams
- **Best New Artist**: **Macklemore & Ryan Lewis**
- **Best Pop Vocal Album**: **"Unorthodox Jukebox"** – Bruno Mars

2015

- **Album of the Year**: **"1989"** – Taylor Swift
- **Song of the Year**: **"Thinking Out Loud"** – Ed Sheeran
- **Record of the Year**: **"Uptown Funk"** – Mark Ronson featuring Bruno Mars
- **Best New Artist**: **Meghan Trainor**
- **Best Pop Vocal Album**: **"In the Lonely Hour"** – Sam Smith

2016

- **Album of the Year: "25"** – Adele
- **Song of the Year: "Thinking Out Loud"** – Ed Sheeran
- **Record of the Year: "Uptown Funk"** – Mark Ronson featuring Bruno Mars
- **Best New Artist: Chance the Rapper**
- **Best Pop Vocal Album: "1989"** – Taylor Swift

2017

- **Album of the Year: "25"** – Adele
- **Song of the Year: "Hello"** – Adele
- **Record of the Year: "Hello"** – Adele
- **Best New Artist: Chance the Rapper**
- **Best Pop Vocal Album: "25"** – Adele

2018

- **Album of the Year: "24K Magic"** – Bruno Mars
- **Song of the Year: "That's What I Like"** – Bruno Mars

- **Record of the Year**: "24K Magic" – Bruno Mars
- **Best New Artist: Alessia Cara**
- **Best Pop Vocal Album**: "24K Magic" – Bruno Mars

2019

- **Album of the Year**: "Golden Hour" – Kacey Musgraves
- **Song of the Year**: "This Is America" – Childish Gambino
- **Record of the Year**: "This Is America" – Childish Gambino
- **Best New Artist: Billie Eilish**
- **Best Pop Vocal Album**: "Sweetener" – Ariana Grande

2020

- **Album of the Year**: "When We All Fall Asleep, Where Do We Go?" – Billie Eilish

- **Song of the Year**: "**Bad Guy**" – Billie Eilish
- **Record of the Year**: "**Bad Guy**" – Billie Eilish
- **Best New Artist: Billie Eilish**
- **Best Pop Vocal Album**: "**Norman Fucking Rockwell!**" – Lana Del Rey

---

Key Statistics and Fun Facts

- **Most Grammy Wins in a Single Year**: **Michael Jackson** and **Carlos Santana** each won **8 Grammy Awards** in a single year (Michael Jackson in 1984 and Carlos Santana in 1999).

- **Most Grammy Wins of All Time: Georg Solti**, a Hungarian-British conductor, holds the record for the most Grammy wins, with **31** Grammy Awards across his career.

- **First Woman to Win Album of the Year**: **Barbra Streisand** became the first woman to win **Album of the Year** in 1966 for her album **"People"**.

- **Youngest Artist to Win Album of the Year**: **Billie Eilish** holds the record for being the youngest artist to win **Album of the Year**, which she accomplished in 2020 for her album **"When We All Fall Asleep, Where Do We Go?"** at the age of 18.

- **Most Wins by a Female Artist**: **Beyoncé** holds the title of the most Grammy wins by a female artist, with **28** Grammy Awards.

- **Most Nominations in Grammy History**: **Quincy Jones** holds the record for the most Grammy nominations, with a total of **80 nominations** over his legendary career.

- **First Grammy Award Ceremony**: The first **Grammy Awards** ceremony took place on **May 4, 1959**, at the Beverly Hilton Hotel in Beverly Hills, California. The event celebrated the achievements of the **1958** music season.

- **Most Nominations in a Single Year**: **Michael Jackson** set the record for the most Grammy nominations in a single year, with **12 nominations** in **1984**.

- **Grammy Awards Broadcast**: The Grammy Awards ceremony is broadcast live on CBS every year and has been viewed by millions worldwide, with a significant following on social media platforms as well.

Made in the USA
Las Vegas, NV
05 March 2025

19122059R00073